SMILEY

JOKE BOOK

SCHOLASTIC

Introduction

Welcome to the Smiley Joke Book! Here you'll find jokes and funny stories written entirely in emoticons. You can work out the meanings yourself or test your family and friends by sending them a Smiley message.

Reading in emoticons might seem tricky to begin with, but it's easy once you get the hang of it. If you get stuck, look at the bottom of each page for clues. You can also turn to the back of the book where you will find a handy Smiley Dictionary.

Tips

Three of the same symbol or the same type of symbol in a row signify a plural:

   girls

    sports

An emoticon can mean exactly what it looks like!

 Why?

 English

Clever combinations of Smileys can help you to express something:

  "Ribbit!" or "Croak!"

 What do you call…

Contents

To help get you started

**Here are some key Smileys explained
to help you get going.**

? what or when   because   "Which?"

 happy, hooray, like, won   boo!, dislike, lost, unhappy

 bad, can't, crossed with, don't, no, not, stop, wrong

 check, good, right, start, yes   you   in, on

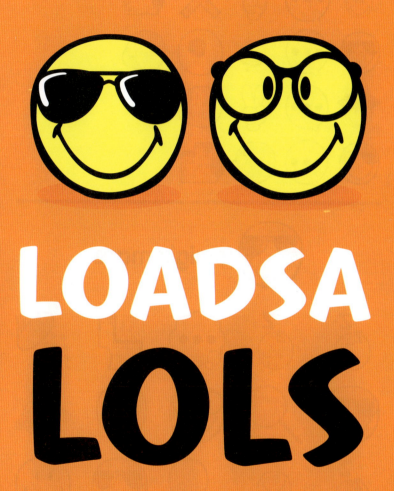

LOADSA
LOLS

Too 😎 for 🏫

😎's nightmare

  sick dreaming scream mirror

A week in the life of

Monday: Friday:

Tuesday: Saturday:

Wednesday: Sunday:

Thursday:

 's birthday

 birthday   day   post

A round of applause

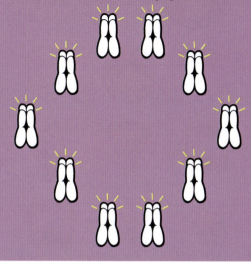

 's to-do list

---

 doorbell   work   party   **11**

's Saturday

's Sunday

   journey   home

 feels the heat

 **has a dream**

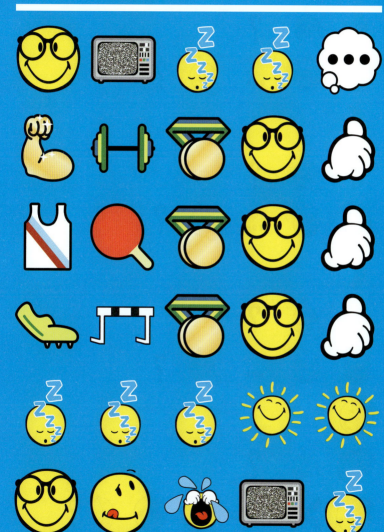

■■■ pause

●●● say, say to

 **goes for ice cream**

 ?

 **?**

 twins   angry    like, love

Q  **?**

A ✗ too -y

Q  **?**

A

Q  **?**

A

A day in the life of

  wide awake   school

A week in the life of

Monday: **Friday:**

Tuesday: **Saturday:**

Wednesday: **Sunday:**

Thursday:

      ?

   @ **&**

 ?

 at night or late alarm **23**

and the zombies

  zombie   badminton

Some  jokes

---

Q ?  ?

A

Q  ?

A -fordshire

Q ?  ?

A

 tells a joke

 ?

 **?**

ping pong   hurdles

 's sports day

SPORTY
JOKES

player in, on rich alley cricket

Q

A

Q

A

Q

A

Q

A

  jog wrap pig, hog end

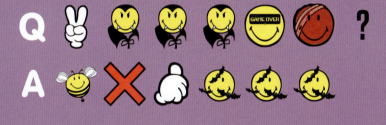

SPOOKY!

song   **ABC** spell   eat   frost

 36

A halloween story

Q 🌍 👻 ✈️ 🏖️ **?**

A BOO (Barbados face)

Q **?** 🎵 🧟 ❤️ **?**

A 🎁 **-ing**

Q **?** 📱 🎃 🏖️ **?**

A 🥪 (witch smiley)

Q **?** 📱 👻 ✖️ (cat smiley) **?**

A (scared smiley) (cat smiley)

Q **?** 📱 (witch smiley) ✖️ ⛄ **?**

A ❄️ **ABC**

/🍬 **trick or treat**   (Barbados face) **Barbados**   (scared smiley) **scared**   **39**

A halloween to-do list

bagel   look, see

The haunted

POO, POO, POO

Q ? 📱 🐶 🚽 ?

A A 💩 -dle

Q ✌️ 🏴󠁧󠁢󠁥󠁮󠁧󠁿 🎓😊 ⏰ ⏰ ⏰ 🚽 ?

A 🐝 🎓😊 💗 📖 💩 -ems

Q ✌️ 😎 🎁 🚽 📰 ?

A 🐝 😎 🦋 💩 -er

Q 🧙😊 💩 👃 ✊ 🌼 🌼 🌼 ?

A sham- 💩

Q ? ⚾ ⚽ 🏀 💩 💗 ?

A

A fiery tale

 writing   smells like   good idea

Q

A

Q

A  -ed

Q

A  -ed

Q

A

 fairy    stink

A week in the life of

Monday:

Tuesday:

Wednesday:

Thursday:

Friday:

Saturday:

Sunday:

  ?

  ?

Name that

Next time you do a take a look in the to see if you can spot any of these.

  : **When you need a** **but nothing comes out**

  : **A very long**

  : **A very rare**

  : **A really good-looking**

  foxy

: A very satisfying

: When you've eaten too many

: A that felt like it came out sideways

: A that takes a long time

: When you do lots of little

 burning hot

49

💩's sports day

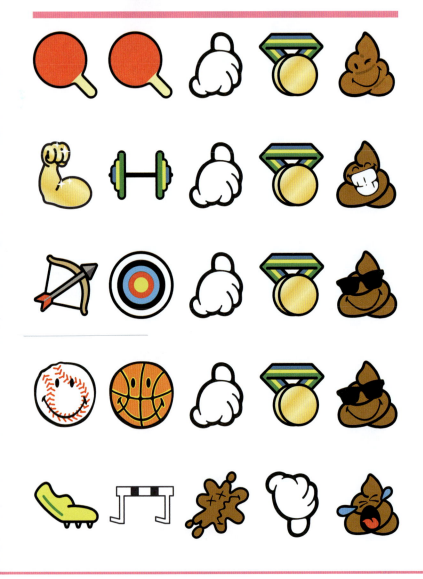

 ping pong

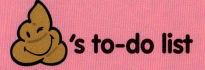

 won   lost

SAY
WHAT?!

Can you figure out these Smiley sayings? Check your answers on page 96.

1

2

3

---

 knock   wood   to

4

_____

_____

5

_____

_____

6

_____

_____

7

_____

_____

8

9

---

 toss   nose, smell   beat   bush

10

11

12

 run   foot

13

_____

_____

14

_____

_____

15   &

_____

_____

 check   make

16

_____

_____

17

_____

_____

 like   **?** might   fly

59

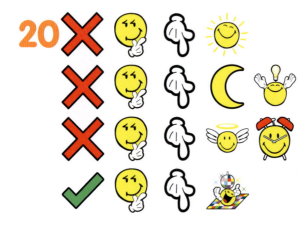

18

_____

_____

19

_____

_____

20

_____

_____

  best   blame   later

21

_____

_____

22

_____

_____

23

24

25

26

  work   hard   deer   rat

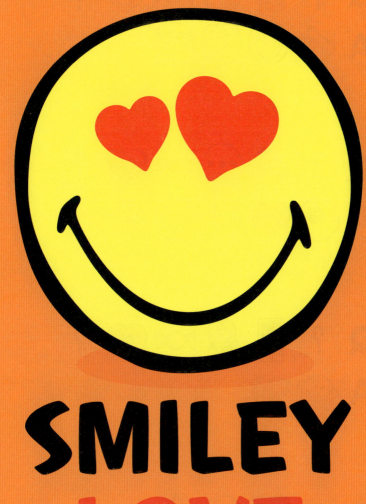

SMILEY
LOVE

Q

Q

Q

Q

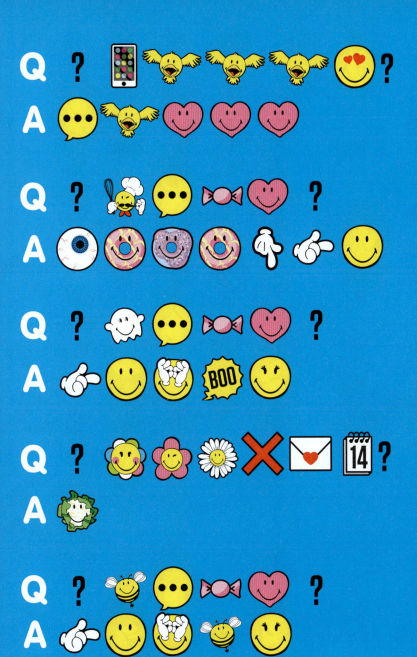

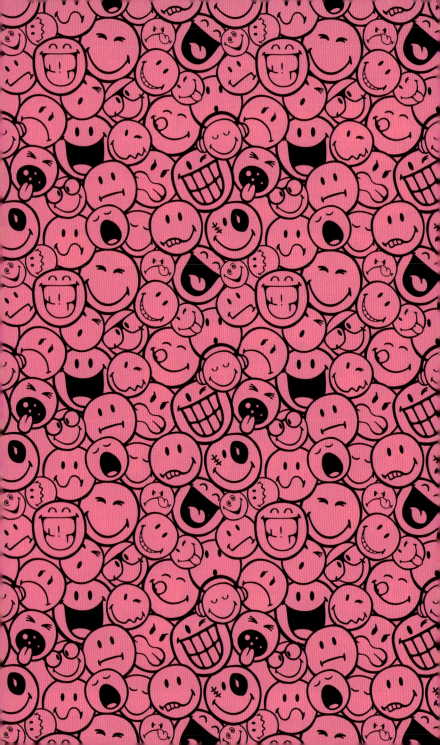

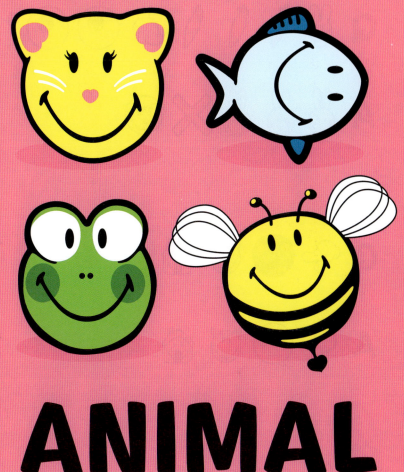

ANIMAL
JOKES

  neigh-bourhood squeak nut

Q

A

Q

A

Q

A

What do you get...

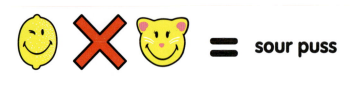 = sour puss

 = pork chop

 = lamb chop

 = chip shop

 = bunny ribbit

 = milk & quackers

✗ crossed with 🎵🐟 tuna fish 😎 swim

Q

A

Q

A

Q

A

Q ?  ?

A

Q  ?

A

Q ? ?

A

Q

A

Q

A

Q

A

crisp rugby

Q ?  ?

A

Q ?  ?

A

Q ?  ?

A

sunburnt, hot   can't see

Q ?  ?

A

Q ?  ?

A

Q ?  ?

A

 live

Q ?  ?

A

Q ?  ?

A

Q ?  ?

A

Q ?

A

croak

Happy
HOLIDAYS!

Q ?  ?

A ?

Q

A

Q

A

 tape · steam · because

Q

A

Q

A

Q

A

Q

A

's Christmas day

    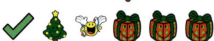

  Christmas   **snowball**

Q

A

Q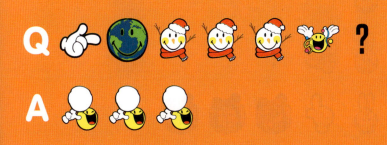

A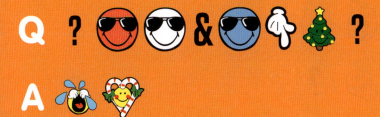

Q ? 😎😎 & 😎 ☝ 🎄 ?

A

Q ? 🎄 💬 😭 💡 ?

A

 candy cane   wrapping   up

?

 **?**

 ?

 ?

  wise man

's Christmas Eve to-do list

 Christmas stocking

Q ?  ?

A

Q ? 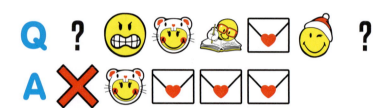 ?

A ![X] ![mouse face] ![envelope with heart] ![envelope with heart] ![envelope with heart]

![envelope with heart] cards   ![laughing face] bite

The  dictionary

Here's a dictionary to help you identify some of the more difficult or unusual Smileys. You'll also find here explanations for some of the trickier combinations.

Main dictionary

 alarm

 beat

 blushing, embarrassed

 alley

 because

 boo, dislike, lost, unhappy

 angry

 doorbell

 boogie

 artist

 best

 Bulgaria

 badminton

 birthday

 burning hot

 bagel

 bite

 bush, tree

 Barbados

 blame

 call, phone

cards, post

 crying, sad

 fairy

 cauliflower

 day

 fly

 chef, make

 deer

 foot

 Christmas

 diamond, hard

 foxy

 Christmas stocking

 doze

 French

 clean

 dream, dreaming

 friend

 crackers

 driving me

 frost, ice, snowflake

 cricket

 eat

 ghost, ghoul

 crisp

 end, game over

 gift, wrap, wrapping

 bad, can't, crossed with, don't, no, not, stop, wrong

 English

go to, to

 check, good, right, start, yes

 knock

 nothing, silent

 good idea

 late, night

 nut

 happy

 listen

 parp

 happy, hooray, like, won

 live

 party

 hear, listen

 look, see

 pig, hog

 I, I'm

 mirror

 player

 in love

 money

 road

 in, on

 mummy

 rich

 jog, run

 naughty

 rugby

 joke

 New York

 runner, sprinter

 journey

 nose, smells, stinks

 same, twins

92

 say, say to

 scared

 scream

 school

 sick

 Singapore

 sleep

 snowball

 song

 ABC spell

 steam

 stormy

 story

 swim

 tape

 teacher

 thoughtful

 throw

 trick

 tune, music

 up

 vampire

 water

 what, when

 who?

 wide awake

 wise man

 which, witch

why

work, writing, school lesson

zombie

Combinations

  archery

  holiday

  beautiful

   insects

  beautiful

   knock knock

  baa

   later

  can't see

  leap

  croak, ribbit!

  looking good

  elf-esteem

  moo

  girls

 moonlight

   hiss

neigh-bourhood

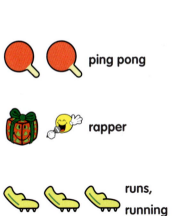 ping pong

🎵 🐟 tuna fish

🎁 🗣️ rapper

💬 🐦 tweet

👟👟👟 runs, running

✉️ 📅14 Valentine's Day

👃 💨 smells like

💪 🏋️ weightlifting

⚽🏏🏀 sport

❓ 📱 what do you call

🍬❤️ sweetheart

👉🌍 where

💬🐭 squeak

😊❓ who's there

🏠🐴 stable

🌳🌳🌳 wood

😛/🍬 trick or treat

👉😊 you

Say What!? Answers

1 = Knock on wood.

2 = I don't sleep, I dream.

3 = Barking up the wrong tree.

4 = Elvis has left the building.

5 = Listen and silent are written with the same letters.

6 = Wake up and smell the roses.

7 = See eye to eye.

8 = Don't beat around the bush.

9 = Under the weather.

10 = This guy.

11 = A toss-up.

12 = Why do noses run and feet smell?

13 = I love seafood, I see food and eat it!

14 = Rain check.

15 = Make like a tree and leave.

16 = Raining cats and dogs.

17 = Pigs might fly.

18 = See you later.

19 = Best of both worlds.

20 = Blame it on the boogie.

21 = Over the moon.

22 = Out of the blue.

23 = No idea.

24 = Work hard for money.

25 = Smell you later.

26 = I smell a rat.